my first book of questions and answers

medieval times

Maggie Brown

p

This is a Parragon Book
First published in 2002

Parragon
Queen Street House
4 Queen Street
Bath BA1 1HE, UK

Produced by

David West 🧍🧍 Children's Books
7 Princeton Court
55 Felsham Road
Putney
London SW15 1AZ

British Library Cataloguing-in-Publication Data

A catalogue record for this book is available from
the British Library.

Hardback ISBN 0-75257-568-6
Paperback ISBN 0-75257-574-0

Printed in China

Designers
Aarti Parmar, Rob Shone, Fiona Thorne

Illustrators
Chris Brown, Graham Kennedy (Allied Artists)

Cartoonist
Peter Wilks (SGA)

Editor
James Pickering

CONTENTS

4 When were the Middle Ages?

4 Who were the barbarians?

5 Who was Charlemagne?

6 Who were smash-and-grab raiders?

7 Where did the Vikings come from?

7 How long was a Viking longship?

8 Did all Vikings go on raids?

8 Which lands did the Vikings travel to?

9 Where was Vinland?

10 What sort of things happened at a Thing?

10 How many letters were there in the Viking alphabet?

11 What do the Vikings have to do with Wednesdays?

12 Who were the Normans?

13 What were the first castles like?

14 How did enemies lay siege to castles?

15 Where were the dungeons?

16 Were castles built outside Europe?

16 Did Americans build castles?

17 Where was Great Zimbabwe?

18 Who wore metal suits?

19 What did knights do in peacetime?

20 Which French peasant girl led an army?

20 Who was Genghis Khan?

21 Who were the knights of the Round Table?

22 Why did people go on Crusades?

22 What was the Black Death?

23 Why did the peasants rebel?

24 Who was a teenage traveller?

24 Who spent 28 years on the road?

25 Who first explored the South Pacific Ocean?

26 Where was the land of the four quarters?

27 Why were the Incas great?

27 Why did the Incas get knotted?

28 Who built a city in a lake?

28 Who fought Flower Wars?

29 Why didn't Aztec warriors kill their enemies?

30 Who were the conquistadors?

31 Who led the conquistadors?

31 What helped the conquistadors win?

32 Index

? When were the Middle Ages?

The Middle Ages were the years between the ancient and modern worlds in western Europe. They began when the Romans were conquered by invading Germanic tribes during the 5th century, and lasted for about 1,000 years.

Barbarian invasion of Rome

Germanic warriors

? Who were the barbarians?

The Romans thought the invaders were rough and uncivilized, so they called them barbarians. The barbarians broke the Romans' vast Western Empire into small kingdoms.

❓ Who was Charlemagne?

Charlemagne was one of the most magnificent rulers of the Middle Ages. By his death in 814, he'd built up the biggest empire since Roman times.

Charlemagne's empire didn't last long, though. It was also attacked by invaders and, in the 840s, his grandsons divided it in three.

Charlemagne

TRUE OR FALSE?

England wasn't invaded.

FALSE. England was invaded by the Angles, Saxons and Jutes. The name England means 'the land of the Angles'.

Charlemagne's father was called Pepin the Short.

TRUE. And one of Charlemagne's grandsons was called Charles the Bald.

? Who were smash-and-grab raiders?

Viking warriors

On 8 June, 793, Viking warriors made a lightning attack on the monastery of Lindisfarne (an island off England's northeastern coast), killing some of the monks and stealing their treasure. This was the first Viking raid we know of, but not the last – for the next 300 or so years, Viking warriors were among the most feared in Europe.

?Where did the Vikings come from?

The Viking homelands were in Scandinavia, in the countries we now call Denmark, Norway and Sweden – a long sea journey from Lindisfarne. The chief secret of the Vikings' success was their brilliance at shipbuilding and sailing.

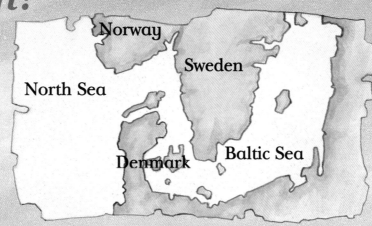

North Sea

Norway

Sweden

Denmark

Baltic Sea

?How long was a Viking longship?

Longship

Viking longships weren't all that big. The largest ships carried 50 warriors and, at 28 m long, they were about six times the length of a modern-day sea kayak.

7

TRUE OR FALSE?

Viking warriors wore helmets. with horns.

FALSE. Old books and movies show fancy horned helmets, but real Viking helmets were fairly plain.

The scariest Viking warriors were called 'berserks'.

TRUE. They were utterly fearless, and wore bearskin cloaks to give themselves a bear's strength.

? Did all Vikings go on raids?

Despite their frightening reputation, very few Vikings were raiders. Most travellers were looking for new goods to buy or lands to settle. Others stayed at home, where country people made a living from farming or fishing, while townsfolk did jobs like shopkeeping or metalwork.

? Which lands did the Vikings travel to?

The Vikings were an adventurous lot who travelled as far east as Russia, and as far south as Africa. They also reached western lands that no European had ever seen – Iceland, Greenland and North America.

Vikings in Vinland

❓ *Where was Vinland?*

When Viking explorer Leif Eriksson landed in eastern North America in 1001, he named the country Vinland after its grapevines. The Vikings met their match in America, though – the Native Americans saw them off within a few years.

Some Viking rulers were buried inside their ships.

TRUE. Along with goods for the Afterlife, including their slaves who were killed and buried as well.

No one is certain where Vinland was.

TRUE. But the most likely site seems to be in the part of Canada we now call Newfoundland.

What sort of things happened at a Thing?

A Thing was a special meeting held by Viking freemen. It was when they passed laws, judged criminals and discussed important issues like whether or not to go to war.

Carving runes

How many letters were there in the Viking alphabet?

The Vikings used special letters called runes to carve messages into wood, stone or bone. There were just 16 runes, but reading a Viking message could be tricky, as some runes stood for more than one sound!

? *What do the Vikings have to do with Wednesdays?*

Some of our days are named after Viking gods. Wednesday comes from Woden, the chief god. Tuesday comes from Tyr (the god of war), Thursday from Thor (the god of thunder), and Friday from Frigg (Woden's wife).

Tyr

Woden

Thor

Frigg

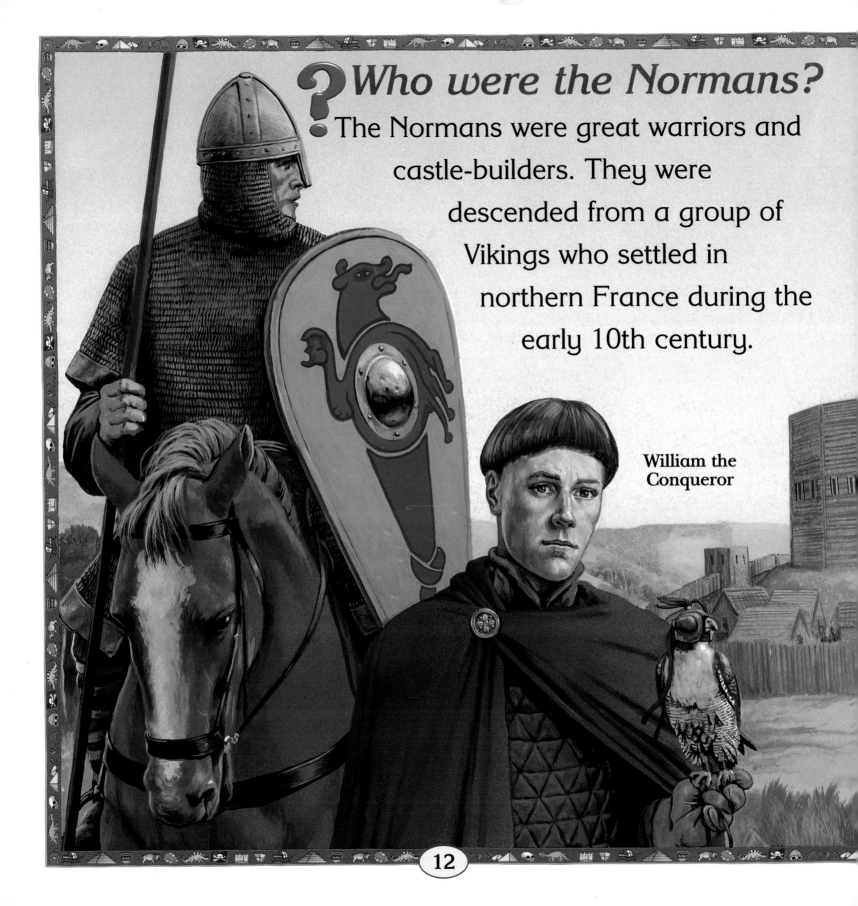

?Who were the Normans?

The Normans were great warriors and castle-builders. They were descended from a group of Vikings who settled in northern France during the early 10th century.

William the Conqueror

? What were the first castles like?

Castles were being built in Europe by the 850s. Most early Norman ones were little more than a wooden tower perched on top of a mound of earth called a motte. Below the motte there was an area called the bailey, where local people took shelter in wartime. As time went on, bigger and bigger castles were built from stone.

❓ How did enemies lay siege to castles?

One way was to surround the castle with an army and wait for the people inside to run out of food and water – and give in. The other way was to fight your way over or through the walls. Some attack weapons were enormous. A mangonel was a huge catapult, for example, while a springald was a gigantic crossbow.

Mangonel

? *Where were the dungeons?*

Prisoners were locked up in dark, damp, smelly dungeons deep beneath a castle tower. It was almost impossible to escape.

Dungeon

TRUE OR FALSE?

Stone castle staircases spiralled up to the right.

TRUE. This meant a right-handed enemy knight fighting upwards had trouble using his sword.

Castles didn't have toilets.

FALSE. Toilets were usually a hole high up in the walls – everything dropped into the moat or a smelly cesspit.

Japanese castle

❓ Were castles built outside Europe?

They certainly were – lots were built in the Middle East and in Japan. Japanese castles were bases for warriors called samurai.

Pueblo Bonito

❓ Did Americans build castles?

Some of the towns built by the Anasazi people of North America were like a cross between a castle and an apartment block. The biggest, Pueblo Bonito, was D-shaped, with its outer walls formed by four-storey-high buildings.

Great
Zimbabwe

❓*Where was Great Zimbabwe?*

Great Zimbabwe was the mighty capital city of the Shona people of East Africa. At the city's heart was an area surrounded by stone walls, which were as thick and strong as a castle's.

The samurai invented judo.

TRUE. Judo developed from jujitsu, a much rougher sport practised by samurai.

Some ships had castles.

TRUE. In the Middle Ages, some warships had mini-turrets called castles, at the front and back.

Who wore metal suits?

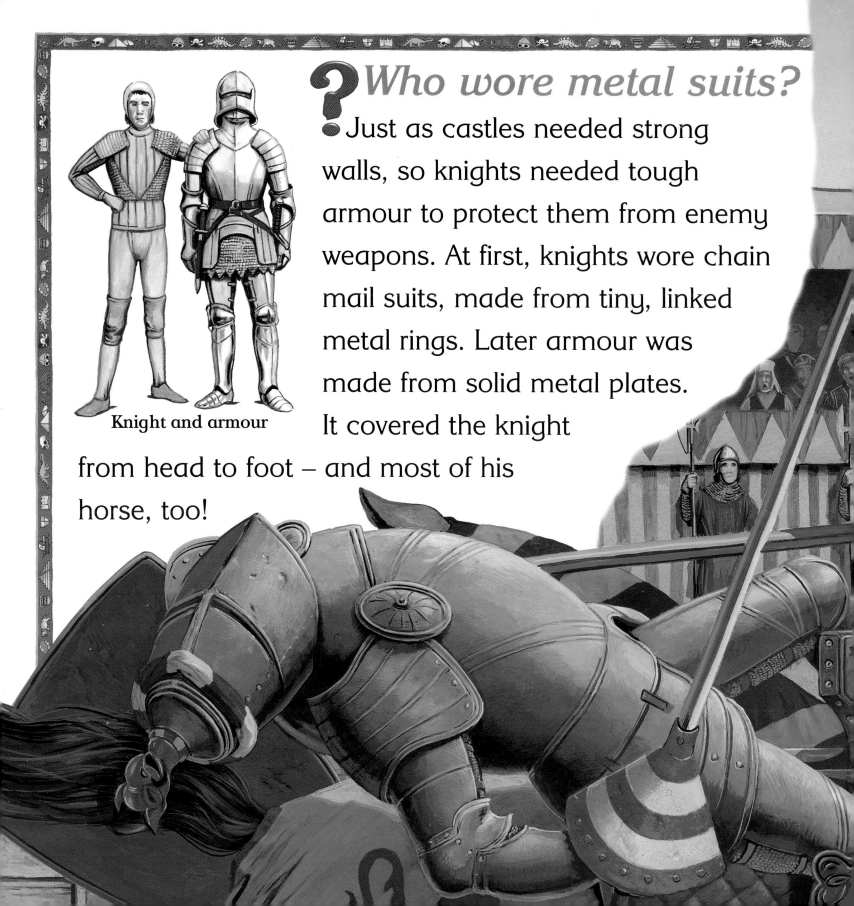

Just as castles needed strong walls, so knights needed tough armour to protect them from enemy weapons. At first, knights wore chain mail suits, made from tiny, linked metal rings. Later armour was made from solid metal plates. It covered the knight from head to foot – and most of his horse, too!

Knight and armour

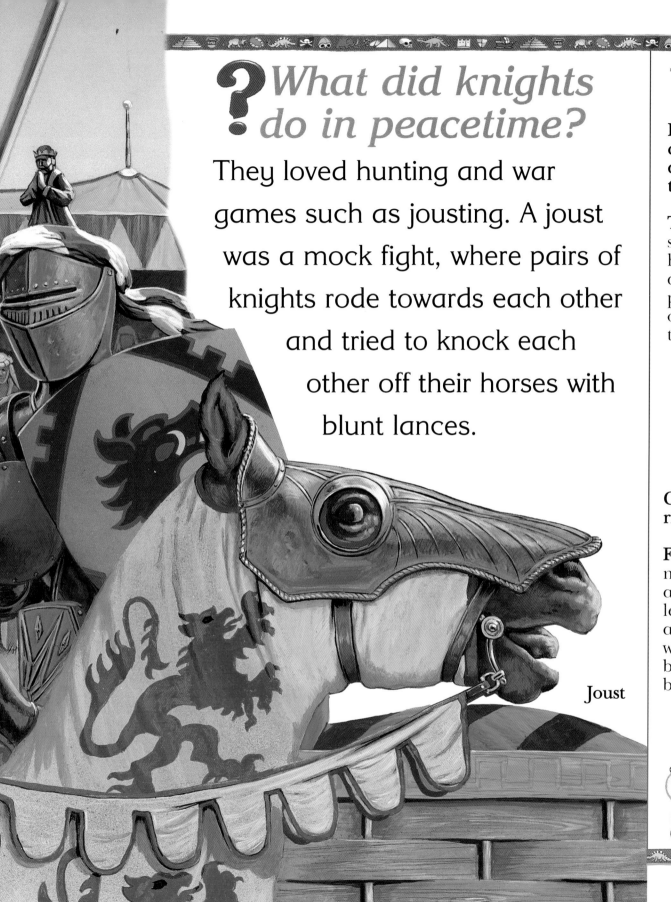

? *What did knights do in peacetime?*

They loved hunting and war games such as jousting. A joust was a mock fight, where pairs of knights rode towards each other and tried to knock each other off their horses with blunt lances.

Joust

Which French peasant girl led an army?

Joan of Arc lived during the Hundred Years' War between France and England. In 1429, when she was about 17, the French king gave her an army which she led to victory in many battles against the English. But two years later, she was captured and burnt at the stake.

Joan of Arc

Genghis Khan

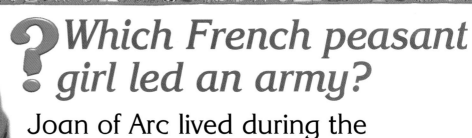

Who was Genghis Khan?

Genghis Khan ruled the Mongol people of Asia. By his death in 1227, he had conquered the largest land empire the world has ever known – stretching from Russia to China.

Search for the Holy Grail

？ *Who were the knights of the Round Table?*

The people of the Middle Ages loved stories about King Arthur, Sir Lancelot and the other knights of the Round Table. The knights' biggest adventure was their search for the Holy Grail, the cup that Jesus is supposed to have used during the Last Supper.

Why did people go on Crusades?

The Crusades were holy wars fought by Christians, mainly to capture Palestine (the land where Jesus had lived) from the Muslims. About 40,000 Christians went on the First Crusade in 1096 – from kings and knights, to townspeople and peasants.

What was the Black Death?

This was a terrible plague which swept through Asia and Europe during the mid-14th century, killing millions of people. Back in the Middle Ages, no one knew what caused it or how to treat it. But we now know the plague was carried by rat fleas, which passed the disease on if they bit people.

Crusade battle

❓ *Why did the peasants rebel?*

Peasants were the lowest of the low in the Middle Ages. The worst-off were slaves, while the rest farmed the land and paid taxes of money or food to their lord. By the mid-14th century, some peasants had had enough and there were riots and rebellions throughout Europe.

Rebelling peasants

Who was a teenage traveller?

Marco Polo was only 17 in 1271, when he set sail from Italy on a trading expedition with his father and uncle. Their ship landed in North Africa, then they headed east overland on camels. Four years later they reached China.

Marco Polo

Who spent 28 years on the road?

Ibn Battuta in India

The famous Arab traveller Ibn Battuta began his adventures in 1325 when he was 21 years old. By the time he hung up his walking sandals he had covered 120,000 km, travelling as far east as Sumatra, and as far south as the Mali Empire in Africa.

? Who first explored the South Pacific Ocean?

The Polynesian peoples of the South Pacific were among the bravest explorers of all time, sailing thousands of kilometres across the ocean in small canoes. They were the first to discover New Zealand, settling there as early as the 9th century.

Polynesian explorers

People thought the world was flat in the Middle Ages.

TRUE. Sailors were frightened of travelling too far, in case they fell off the edge of the world.

Land explorers travelled in caravans.

TRUE. But they weren't like the mobile homes of today. A caravan was a group of travellers and their animals.

? *Where was the land of the four quarters?*

By the late 15th century, the lands of the Inca people of South America stretched for thousands of kilometres. The Incas called their vast empire Tawantinsuyu, which means 'land of the four quarters'.

Incas in battle

Why were the Incas great?

The Incas won their huge empire because they were brilliant warriors and rulers. They governed their lands from magnificent stone cities, linked by more than 25,000 km of roads.

Inca ruler

Why did the Incas get knotted?

The Incas didn't have a written language – they recorded things by tying knots in long pieces of string. The records were called quipus, from the Inca word for 'knot', and the biggest had more than 2,000 strings.

TRUE OR FALSE?

The Incas called their capital city 'the navel of the world'.

TRUE. That's what the name of the Incas' capital Cuzco means, when it's translated into English.

The Incas didn't build bridges.

FALSE. They lived in the mountains, so they made rope bridges over canyons and gorges.

? Who built a city in a lake?

The Aztecs lived at the same time as the Incas, ruling over an empire in Central America. Their capital, Tenochtitlan, was on an island in the middle of a lake, and its main highways were canals.

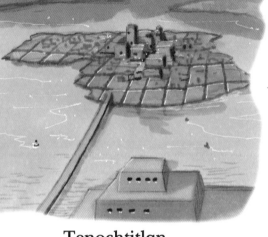

Tenochtitlan

Aztec warriors

? Who fought Flower Wars?

On the day they were born, Aztec boys were given toy bows and arrows. They learnt to fight at school, and when they were 18 they took part in a special battle called a Flower War – fighting with real weapons, not flowers!

? Why didn't Aztec warriors kill their enemies?

The aim of Aztec battles was to capture prisoners and take them back to Tenochtitlan, where priests killed them as a sacrifice to the gods. Human sacrifice may sound bloodthirsty to us, but the Aztecs believed that people who died in this way would be sure of a happy life after death.

？Who were the conquistadors?

Conquistador is a Spanish word for 'conqueror', and the conquistadors were Spanish soldiers and adventurers who invaded Central and South America during the early 16th century. Thousands of Incas and Aztecs were slaughtered by the conquistadors, and their civilizations destroyed.

Conquistadors

Who led the conquistadors?

The most famous conquistador leaders were Hernan Cortes and Francisco Pizarro. Cortes's soldiers conquered the Aztecs in 1521, while Pizarro's troops defeated the Incas in the 1530s.

Cortes   Pizarro

What helped the conquistadors win?

The conquistadors were a long way from home, and greatly outnumbered. But unlike the Incas and Aztecs, the Spaniards had guns, and they fought by killing people, not capturing them.

TRUE OR FALSE?

Conquistadors brought the first horses to the Americas.

TRUE. There were no horses in North or South America before the conquistadors brought theirs.

Conquistadors also brought potatoes to South America.

FALSE. Potatoes were first grown in South America, and the conquistadors were the first Europeans to eat them.

Index

Anasazi 16

armour 18

Arthur, King 21

Aztecs 28–29, 30, 31

barbarians 4

Battuta, Ibn 24

Black Death 22

castle 12–17

Charlemagne 5

conquistador 30–31

Cortes, Hernan 31

Crusades 22

Eriksson, Leif 9

exploration 8–9, 24–25

Genghis Khan 20

Great Zimbabwe 17

Hood, Robin 21

Incas 26–27, 30, 31

Joan of Arc 20

jousting 19

judo 17

knight 18–19, 21

Lancelot 21

longship 7

mangonel 14

Middle Ages 4

Normans 12–13

peasant 23

Pizarro, Francisco 31

Polo, Marco 24

Pueblo Bonito 16

Romans 4

Round Table 21

runes 10

samurai 16, 17

ship 7, 9, 17, 25

Shona 17

siege 14

springald 14

Thing 10

Vikings 6–11, 12

Vinland 9

warrior 6, 7, 12, 16, 26, 28, 29, 31